This Book is Presented to:

Jack

From:

Mom

3

05 04 03 02 01   10 9 8 7 6 5 4 3 2 1

David and God's Covenant—
Scriptural Stories Based on God's Unbreakable Promises
Covenant Kids

ISBN 1-57794-298-1
Copyright © 2001 by Harrison House

Published by Harrison House, Inc.
P.O. Box 35035
Tulsa, Oklahoma 74153

Written by Susan Janos.
Illustrations by Lisa Browning.
Printed and bound in Belgium.

DAVID AND GOD'S COVENANT

Scriptural Stories Based on God's Unbreakable Promises

COVENANT KIDS

Harrison House Tulsa, Oklahoma

Dear Parent,

We are pleased to bring you the Covenant Kids Series *for children. Each of these books is written to help your children grasp the truths of the Bible at an early age. These truths will help your children as they grow to rely on God's Word for guidance and on the Holy Spirit to lead them through their daily lives.*

In order to ensure these books are biblically accurate, we have listed the exact Scriptures we referenced in writing the text, so that you, as a parent, can refer back to the biblical occurrence of each story. Our desire is that your children will allow the truth of God into their hearts, so that they will never forget its significance in their life. Because of this, we did draw on different books of the Bible to give a full understanding of the scriptural principles.

David and God's Covenant reveals the importance of God's covenant with His children. This truth shows children why we trust in God, no matter what our circumstances may look like. It establishes the Lord God as our Protector, Caregiver, and loving Father, and it reveals how faith works in an easy-to-understand story.

We pray that you and your children will begin to understand the awesome covenant we have received from our Lord and that He will continue to reveal His Word to you as never before.

The Publisher

What is a Covenant?

A covenant is a promise. A covenant with God is a promise that cannot be broken.

God gave two covenants in the Bible, the Old Testament and the New Testament. The Old Testament was given only to the nation of Israel. But, the New Testament is given to anyone who makes Jesus his or her Lord and Savior. (Galatians 3:14.)

The New Testament includes all the promises of the old covenant plus all the promises of the new covenant! God's promises to you include eternal life, righteousness, peace, joy, healing, protection, provision, and much more! (Romans 14:17; John 3:16; 1 Peter 2:24; Psalm 91; Philippians 4:19.) He even gave you the Holy Spirit to help you and be your friend. (John 4:16.) But to have all the promises of the new covenant, you must know what it says and believe that it is true. (Hebrews 11:6.)

The Covenant Kids book series shows you God's covenant promises so that you can put them to work in your life, now and in the future. We encourage you to read this book over and over again. If you will do that, you will begin to memorize God's promises and when trouble comes, you will remember your covenant with God. Remind Him of His promises to you and He will always take care of you.

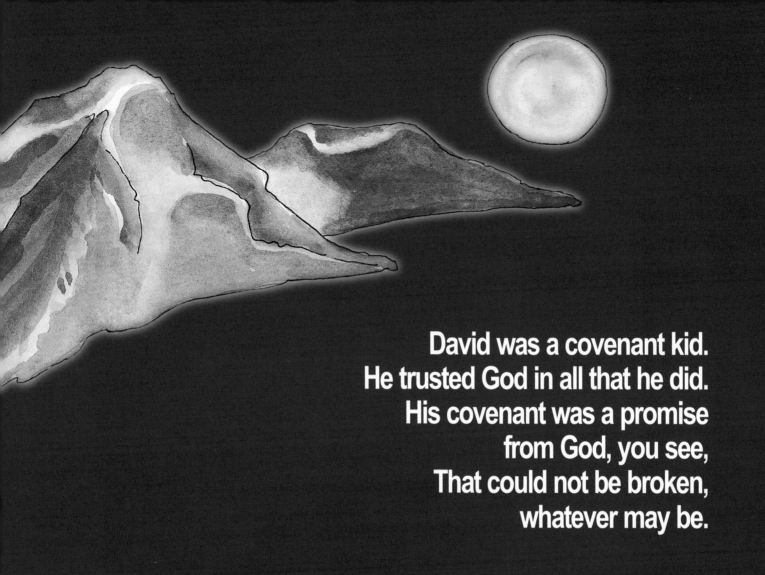

David was a covenant kid.
He trusted God in all that he did.
His covenant was a promise
from God, you see,
That could not be broken,
whatever may be.

My mercy will I keep for him for evermore,
and my covenant shall stand fast with him.
Psalm 89:28

David knew this covenant was sure.
It was a promise from God
That would forever endure.

*My covenant will I not break, nor alter the
thing that is gone out of my lips.* Psalm 89:34

This covenant meant
protection and care
The Lord would provide.
For David, His friend,
The Lord would guide.

I have found David my servant; with my holy oil have I anointed him: With whom my hand shall be established: mine arm also shall strengthen him. Psalm 89:20,21

David was a shepherd boy
  And faithful to watch His Father's sheep.
God helped him to keep them safe,
  And when danger came, up he would leap!

But David went and returned from Saul
to feed his father's sheep at Bethlehem.
1 Samuel 17:15

Now David's brothers
had gone to fight,
For the Philistines
had come with might.

*And the three eldest sons of Jesse went
and followed Saul to the battle....* 1 Samuel 17:13

David's father sent
him to see
How his brothers
were doing
In the king's army.

And Jesse said unto David his son, Take now for thy brethren an ephah of this parched corn, and these ten loaves, and run to the camp...and look how thy brethren fare.... 1 Samuel 17:17,18

When he arrived, Goliath was there,
A big, bad giant yelling everywhere.
"Who will fight me? Who can take me down?
I can beat anyone. I'm the meanest around!"

And as he talked with them, behold, there came up the champion,
the Philistine of Gath, Goliath by name, out of the armies
of the Philistines, and spake according to the same words:
and David heard them. 1 Samuel 17:23

David said,
"How dare he speak
To the armies of God when
A covenant we keep!"

And David spake to the men that stood by him, saying, What shall be done to the man that killeth this Philistine, and taketh away the reproach from Israel? for who is this uncircumcised Philistine, that he should defy the armies of the living God? 1 Samuel 17:26

David spoke before the king,
And he said, "I'll defeat this Philistine."
And said King Saul,
"But you're so small,
And he's so big and mean!"

And David said to Saul, Let no man's heart fail because of him; thy servant will go and fight with this Philistine. And Saul said to David, Thou art not able to go against this Philistine to fight with him: for thou art but a youth, and he a man of war from his youth. 1 Samuel 17:32,33

But when David was young
And keeping the sheep,
Up came a lion,
Creep, creep, creep!

And there came a lion...
and took a lamb out of the flock.
1 Samuel 17:34,35

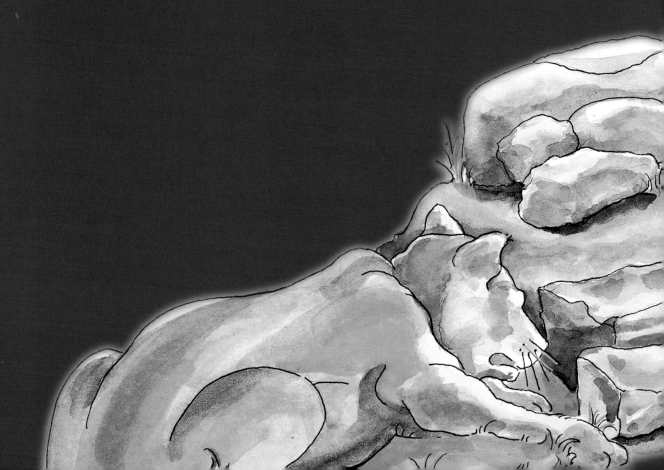

David grabbed him and beat him
With the power of God!
The Lord protected His servant,
Even when the lion clawed.

And I went out after him, and smote him, and
delivered it out of his mouth.... 1 Samuel 17:35

And then a bear tried to attack,
But David knew his covenant
And beat the bear. WHACK!

Thy servant slew both the lion and the bear....
1 Samuel 17:36

And David replied,
"The same as the bear
  this giant will be.
He'll fall like the lion,
For God's covenant
  is with me."

The Lord that delivered me out of the paw of the lion, and out of the paw of the bear, he will deliver me out of the hand of this Philistine. 1 Samuel 17:37

The king said, "All right.
Take my helmet and my sword."
But David replied, "No thanks!
All I need is my sling
and the Lord."

And David girded his sword upon his armour, and he assayed to go; for
he had not proved it. And David said unto Saul, I cannot go with these;
for I have not proved them. And David put them off him. 1 Samuel 17:39

So David took his staff in his hand
And chose five smooth stones
out of the brook.
He put them in a shepherd's bag
And in his hand,
his sling he took.

And he took his staff in his hand, and chose him five smooth stones out of the brook, and put them in a shepherd's bag which he had, even in a scrip; and his sling was in his hand: and he drew near to the Philistine.
1 Samuel 17:40

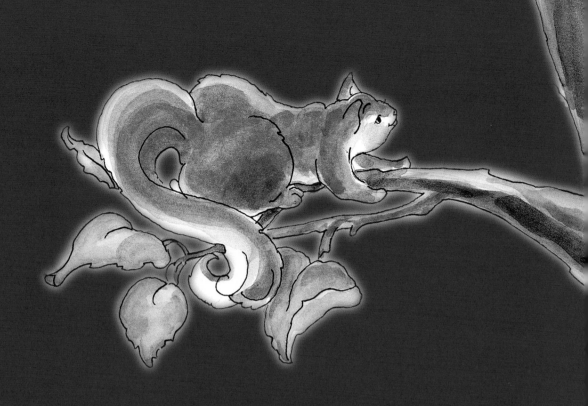

The giant Goliath saw David there
And said, "I'm not a dog so small.
I'm big, bad, and really mad,
And today you're gonna fall!"

*And the Philistine said unto David, Am I a dog, that thou comest to me
with staves? And the Philistine cursed David by his gods.* 1 Samuel 17:43

But David knew the Lord his God
And that His covenant stands.
He said, "The battle is the Lord's,
And He will give you into our hands!"

Then said David to the Philistine, Thou comest to me with a sword,
and with a spear, and with a shield: but I come to thee in the name of
the Lord of hosts, the God of the armies of Israel, whom thou has defied.
This day will the Lord deliver thee into mine hand.... 1 Samuel 17:45,46

As the giant came near,
David ran forward without fear.
And with a swing of his sling,
He gave the stone a fling.

David hasted, and ran
toward the army to meet
the Philistine. And David put
his hand in his bag,
and took thence a stone,
and slang it....
1 Samuel 17:48,49

The stone shot straight and true
And landed with a THUD!
Into Goliath's head it flew,
And he fell down in the mud!

And it smote the Philistine in his forehead...
and he fell upon his face to the earth.
1 Samuel 17:49

Goliath had been beaten
By a shepherd's son.
And just as David had said,
David had won!

*So David prevailed over the Philistine
with a sling and with a stone....* 1 Samuel 17:50

David knew his covenant
was sure.
He trusted God
And by faith, endured.

And David went out whithersoever Saul sent him,
and behaved himself wisely.... 1 Samuel 18:5

God also wants
a covenant with you!
And to ask Jesus
in your heart
Is all you have to do.

That if thou shalt confess with thy mouth the Lord Jesus,
and shalt believe in thine heart that God hath raised him
from the dead, thou shalt be saved. Romans 10:9

Dear Jesus,

I ask You to come
into my heart,

To be my Lord,
to give me a new start.

Thank You for my covenant
that is now sure,

For protection and care,

And for love that endures.

Amen.

Additional copies of this book and other book titles from Harrison House are available from your local bookstore.

Other Children's and Youth Books Published by Harrison House

Covenant Kids - Jesus Our Saviour
Scriptural Stories Based on God's
Unbreakable Promises
Harrison House - Ages 3-7

Prayers That Avail Much® For Kids Vol. 1 & 2
Germaine Copeland - Ages 2-8

365 Confessions For Kids
Scriptural Confessions That Make God
Personal In Little Lives
Virginia Kite - Ages 4 & up

*Commander Kellie and the Superkids*SM *Series*

#1 The Mysterious Presence

#2 The Quest for the Second Half

#3 Escape from Jungle Island

#4 In Pursuit of the Enemy

#5 Caged Rivalry

#6 Mystery of the Missing Junk
Christopher P. N. Maselli - Ages 8-10

HARRISON HOUSE

P. O. Box 35035

Tulsa, Oklahoma 74153

For a complete list of our titles, visit us at our website:
www.harrisonhouse.com